SEA LIONS

by Tanya Lee Stone

BLACKBIRCH®
PRESS

San Diego • Detroit • New York • San Francisco • Cleveland • New Haven, Conn. • Waterville, Maine • London • Munich

For more information, contact
The Gale Group, Inc.
27500 Drake Rd.
Farmington Hills, MI 48331-3535
Or you can visit our Internet site at http://www.gale.com

Photographs © 1994 by Chang Yi-Wen

Illustrations © 1994 by Lin Chuan-Zong

Cover Photograph © Corel

© 1994 by Chin-Chin Publications Ltd.

No. 274-1, Sec.1 Ho-Ping E. Rd., Taipei, Taiwan, R.O.C.
Tel: 886-2-2363-3486 Fax: 886-2-2363-6081

LIBRARY OF CONGRESS CATALOGING-IN-PUBLICATION DATA

Stone, Tanya Lee.
  Sea lions / by Tanya Lee Stone.
    v. cm. -- (Wild wild world)
Includes bibliographical references (p. 24) and index.
Contents: Flippers and tails -- Social sea lions -- Mating -- Sea lion
show-offs.
 ISBN 1-4103-0036-6 (hardback : alk. paper)
1. Sea lions--Juvenile literature. [1. Sea lions.] I. Title. II.
Series.

QL737.P63S76 2003
599.79'75--dc21   2002154168

Printed in Taiwan
10 9 8 7 6 5 4 3 2 1

Table of Contents

Flippers and Tails

Sea lions are marine mammals. That means they are mammals that live much of their lives in the ocean.

Instead of arms and legs, sea lions have flippers for swimming.

On land, a sea lion can walk on all four flippers. Unlike a seal, a sea lion can lift its heavy upper body on its front flippers.

A sea lion's front flippers are curved. Its back flippers are straighter and shorter than its front flippers. Back flippers also have nails.

Sea lions have short tails. They also have visible ears. They are sometimes called eared seals.

5

Life in the
Water

6

Sea lions spend a lot of time swimming. They swim to find food. They eat mainly fish and squid.

Sea lions have pointed heads and smooth, torpedo-shaped bodies that help them swim quickly through the water. A sea lion can swim between 15 and 25 miles per hour!

Unlike seals that steer with their flippers, sea lions steer with their head and neck. They float on their backs to rest in the water.

Sea lions cannot breathe underwater. They come to the surface for air. They have special nostrils that can close to keep water out.

To stay warm in the cold water, sea lions have an oily, waterproof coat underneath their hair. A layer of fat—called blubber—also helps keep them warm.

Sea Lion Sounds

Sea lions are very noisy!

They make a loud barking sound when they talk to each other.

Males generally make more noise than females.

A group of sea lions sounds a lot like a pack of barking dogs!

Social Sea Lions

Sea lions are large creatures. Males can weigh up to 900 pounds and are often 7 feet long. Females are smaller. They weigh between 100 and 250 pounds and can be 6 feet long.

These heavy animals are able to pull themselves onto land with their flippers. This is called hauling out.

Sea lions like to gather in groups. When they rest together on the water, the group is called a raft. On land, a group of sea lions is called a colony. Males tend to gather in separate groups from females.

Sea Lion Sleep

After a long swim, a sea
lion needs its sleep.

Sea lions sleep on land.
While they sleep, they can warm up in
the sun. If it gets too warm, a sea lion
lifts its head up high to cool off.

Sea lions often sleep either very
close together or on top of each other.

12

Mating

Breeding season for sea lions is between May and July. Babies are born about a year later.

During breeding season, a male sea lion claims his territory. He will mate with several females in his territory. An adult sea lion is called a bull. An adult female is called a cow.

To defend its territory and communicate with the cows, a bull barks loudly. A male will bark constantly during this time.

A male will also fight off another male trying to enter his territory.

The breeding area, called a rookery, is very noisy!

Little Pups

A baby sea lion is called a pup. Pups weigh between 15 and 20 pounds at birth and are between 2 and 3 feet long. Pups are born with their eyes open.

A pup will drink its mother's milk for 5 months to a year. The milk is high in protein and helps a pup grow quickly.

A mother sea lion leaves its pup in the colony for a few days at a time while she fishes in the ocean. The pup sleeps and plays with other pups while she is gone.

When she returns, a pup can easily pick its mother out of the group by sight, smell, and the sound of her bark. A cow finds her pup in the same way.

A mother can locate her pup among hundreds of others that look almost exactly alike.

Learning from Mother

A cow teaches her pup how to swim. By 6 weeks old, it is a good swimmer!

Mothers also teach their pups how to dive and fish.

Sometimes, they just like to play and swim together.

By the time a pup is 6 months old, it can hunt for fish on its own.

Sea Lion Show-Offs

Many zoos keep sea lions so that people can learn about these special animals.

Sea lions are very playful. They are also very smart. That makes them easy to train.

Zookeepers can teach sea lions to do all sorts of tricks. These tricks are useful for showing people a sea lion's unique features.

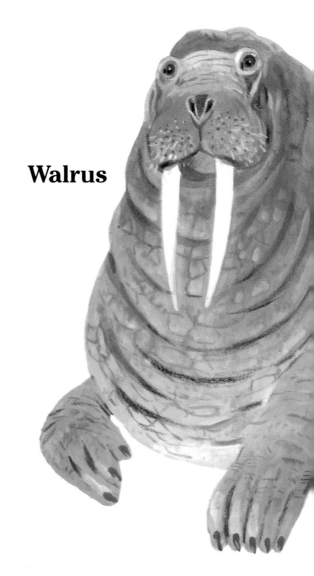

Walrus

Sea Lion Relatives

Seals, including walruses, are related to sea lions.

Walruses look much different than other kinds of seals because of their long tusks.

Unlike sea lions, seals and walruses do not have visible ears. Instead, they have ear holes.

Seals have much smaller front flippers than sea lions. They cannot use them to lift their upper body like sea lions can.

Seals, walruses, and sea lions are all in need of our help to protect their habitat and keep these beautiful animals safe.

Sea Lion

Seal

For More Information

Arnold, Caroline. *Sea Lion.* New York: William Morrow, 1994.

Staub, Frank. *Sea Lions.* Minneapolis, MN: Lerner, 2000.

Walker-Hodge, Judith. *Seals, Sea Lions, and Walruses.* New York: Barrons, 1999.

Glossary

blubber a thick layer of fat underneath the skin

bull an adult male sea lion

colony a group of sea lions on land

cow an adult female sea lion

pup a baby sea lion

raft a group of sea lions on the water